Terracom Poet Series

I0159572

Square Holes

William Driscoll

Terracom Books

Square Holes
Terracom Books Poetry Series/March 2014
First Edition

Published by Terracom Books
A Division of Terracom Media

ISBN–13: 978–0–615–96435–5

Terracom Media

mediaterracom@gmail.com
leopard

CONTENTS

i

A basket, a hat

Three porcelain faces

Bent bamboo to carry his wares

Burdens seldom lightened

A wicker basket, six fen

He needs for food

With three porcelain faces to feed

He recalls their sad geometries

Two chiao for a hat

The bamboo pole not for sale

A wicker basket, six fen

He needs to bury

Three porcelain faces

Straight lines broken thinly

No food needed

To recall their sad geometry

ii

There's something about

a restaurant

after closing

when the lights are dimmed

the tables cleared

and the hollow laughter

that rang so true

is tucked in the beds

of a thousand strangers

one love lies

and boys who do boys

and a little taste of vomit

in the back of the throat

a prelude to the purgation

of loneliness

and dinner drinks

ah, there's a wonder in it!

And who's to say

what's ugly or beautiful

when truth is twisted

so casually

so desperately

Square Holes

garnished and served

with a smile

There's something about

a restaurant

after closing

when the neurotic little men

have scampered home

balding, afraid

and the women

who had cupped

their breasts

hoping for a moment

that would never come

have gone

and everything

is cleared and neat

set and ordered

Except

for the parade of ghosts

who nightly flock

to the empty tables

ordering drink and meat

but are turned away

William Driscoll

There's something about

a restaurant

after closing…

iii

I wrote that out of me

before I understood it

Said the sad old man

eyeing the graying pictures

in a frame… One day… One day…

One day bedazzling to

the senses of even

the senseless wishes

that run and bicker

in the tall grasses

of springtime lullabies

and lazy days

and laughing children

I stood

Senseless and

Bickering and

Lazy and

Laughing

My head straight and tall

My shoulders back easily

(how odd it must have felt

not to stoop forward

like an apostrophe

to a life's plurality

facing backwards)

abcdefg

hijklmnop

qrs... tuv

w... x... y... z

I wrote that out of me

before I understood it

Said the sad old man

eyeing the graying pictures

in a frame... One day... One day...

One day I'll have to throw out

those old pictures...

Inevitability

I no longer desire attainment

without the paths

that lead to its passing

for I've seen the end

briefly

the goal, the rest, the shivering sigh

the light touch that brushes

eternity's quivering thigh

and have returned refreshed

no more ready than a child

to rock away the afternoon

gazing at a field and saying,

"I remember. I remember."

I have come to recall

not learn

what I am

the rye divinity

the densest peace

that joins and stretches

to the bounds of this Universe

and beyond

the deepest darkness

the smallest crawling

blackest thoughts

unacted

that cower in terror

lest their rancid nature

be uncovered for all to see

I am no more flesh than spirit

no less devil than man

it is in doing

blessings

not in deed

indeed

were you to come to me

your arms filled

with all my dearest wishes

I would flee you

the demon

who would steal my tears

and sorrows away…

V

'Grow old...with me' and we'll be
rock–crags that weather the roadside
settling and eroding, yet green in unseen
clefts of the heart, the mind, the soul

together

As the poet wrote long ago
the bedrock of this road we've traveled
is to sigh here and savor that last
'for which the first was made'

young

And we have drunk those years
my love
drunk, so that mountain springs spring
from our being like dancing fountains
of beauty's truths set aside
set aside but not forgotten

forever

Don't fear the years to come my heart
(as many yet to be as we will see)

William Driscoll

plant your roots deep in my veins

deep and drink of all the sorrow

of my yesterday's heartaches and

consume my marrow

to bring forth another spring

vi

There is a beauty in age
advancing courageously
that raises the soul
inward
even as the loins once taut
and moistened then callow
to the light of a clear eye
the curve of a shallow belly
sudden heaving a sallow sigh
of soft caresses
and sweet quivering thighs
sweeping that crescendo
of young energy abounding
spilling over
as a mighty flood
then calming
to a pianissimo conclusion

Trace those tiny lines
to my wizened eye
and wonder
that love still flourishes
in the summer

William Driscoll

in the autumn
in the fall

What can winter
now bring us?
less or more?
when each turn
deepens
our desire
to be inside one skin
of one breath
inward
always inward

Wear me like a coat
against the cold

The Bitch, the Boss and the Buttermen

The shrew

was once

a little girl

too

with wide eyes

sweet as sugar

cane blooming

as a spring

blossom

in the rain

willing to dance

to the music of

a generation

at war with

itself

Breathing poetry

and music

while growing

dreaming of

a love

that fills

the soul

as the sea

rocks the

seabed

Was there

some seed

some sign

some trained eye

might have seen

that her greeds

would grow

so great

her fears

wax

so potent

as to rage

all love

all care

all compassion

to seed?

Dreams can be

deadly when

knives turned

inward

jagged as

the faithless rocks

Square Holes

that score the
hands of timid
climbers

Is bitterness
the answer?
is the world
at large
to blame?

Those…they…
they're the enemy –
why are they all so
cruel to me?

Turning
squirming
on envy's
sharp spit
the shrew waits
in the outer
office
of the aging
corsair
short and graying
fat and suited

William Driscoll

It'll be my turn
today
she spits
or I'll bite the world
I'll rage its blood…

        * * *

The corsair grays
the seas of profit
raiding the land
raping and pillaging
the village people
who admire him
for it

Once he captained
smaller ships
in overflowing
bathtubs splashed
his way through taller
grasses under blue
skies collecting
shiny stones
(he does still)

Square Holes

Was it the bully
in him or the
cowed? whose
to say both
perhaps
that closed his
world distilling
life unto an (un–)
balance(d)
sheet and people
into assets and debits

Narrowing his
roads to one
golden road –
Midas–izing
everything he
touches
minimizing
everything he
once loved
red ink on
the p&l of
his true affections

The boss will
skewer

the shrew

of course

turn her

shriveling talents

to his

unpleasant gain

again

rape her with

word with deed

indeed

finger her

fears and desires

loose change

in his pockets

he'll aggregate her

and collect his interest

(I smell a lawsuit

coming, if nothing

else…)

Unless, of course

she agrees

to kneel

to worship

at the altar of

his transubstantiated

power base

then be swept

aside into

the underpaid corners

of his indifference

Yet before what

does the graying

corsair kneel?

When the robes

are called in

(invariably)

to clean up

the mess

of women

shrewing

and men

dominating

in public

the butter–men

pull the strings

from their

city on a hill

It's to them

the graying corsair

William Driscoll

bends

grabbing his

ankles giving out

with the very stuff

of his self–esteem his

shiny paper stones

and paper profits

The cost of doing

business he

mutters

butter costs money

Grease

the slickers

and they grease

the track to

over–trod the

under trodden

he smirks

on his way

to manicured

links where

millions are made

over dice and drinks

And the children sing:

The Bitch the Boss

and the Butter–men

went to sea in a

wooden shoe…

Misanthrope Party

Misanthropes despise with love

Meddlers love with despite

Materialists love their money

(which can make their coins

stick together)

Join the Misanthrope Party

Dues: Free

Convention: November Annually

Attendance: Highly frowned upon...

Lazy Lions

Lyin' in the sun
Lyin' in the stream
of consciousness'
unconsciousness
sex roams free
where the lioness
hunts the meat
the pact of
the new pack
why does the flesh
taste bland when
tossed at your feet?
the frantic fucking
broken
as a shoddy
Chinese toy?
sleep lazy lion
sleep and dream
of being –
a lioness

a–costic–crostic

fold

up

concentric circles

klash

eschatologically

dawning

under

pendulous

weight

orion's belt

red

lovers mourn

dead babies

xi

There are nine holes

in our bodies

and one that was closed

when we were born

that couples us

to that source

of our body's being

our nourishment

we inhale through these

matter's swirling

shadows and digest

its potent marrows

expelling that

which feeds

eternity's circling

There are six holes

in our soul

and one that was closed

when we were individu–ized

that conjoins us

William Driscoll

to that source

of our being's body

our hidden firma

(the Universe's silent

unsullied whisper)

we pour out our muses

through these holes

like fingerings of a flute

like lover's sighs

where the object

of our love

(that was man or woman)

becomes both

and if our music

is simple enough

that seventh hole

opens again

and we are human

River Views

My love

for you

is

a dementia

that sees

nothing

but your

curt phrases

the curve

of your

parenthesis the

undercurrent

of your

personification's

witness

that stillness

'twixt

one line's

fancy one

fallacious

fractious

frolicking

foible

must I?

keep

returning?

returning

here?

to your

hell your

your calumny

of abominations

or will you

but close

your veins

your verve

your vanity

and try my

place once

just once

it has wonderful

river views

xiii

Rocking in endless motion
ceaseless, restless, swelling
Ocean courts the Raindrop

To dive beneath the crest
to foam and rile in shallows
to join beneath the waves

Rifling in endless action
slicing, illuminating, cleansing
Lightning courts the Firefly

To flash within the quanta
substrata's magnetic veilance
to burst within the flare

Roiling in endless darkness
billowing, threatening, veiling
Sand Storm courts the Dust Speck

To die within the dying
empty, cold and wanting

To see behind the night sky
stars reflect in lovers' eyes

William Driscoll

where

Ocean courts the Raindrop

Solomon, Sheba

Narcissus the pool

Undressing Change

Slowly I trace
my fingers
down the gentle
curve of her calf
excited each time
as a teen
fumbling
with the back
of a front clasp bra
a prom queen
rising to the
writhing passion
of her boy–lovers'
fill–fulment
I remove one shoe
then the next
before she curls
her legs
back laughing
Rough nylons
hone her brandied
thighs shivering
'neath my touch

William Driscoll

sand each calf

smooth as a lathe

heat–licked

like a lamb–spit

she grabs my

hand and bites

the fleshy part

beneath my thumb

I take the pain

Arching her hips

her dress slips

off so tiny

to begin with

so spare

it crumbles

in my hands

like the dark–

purple skin

of a ripe avocado

uncovering

that rich

green–fruit

to devour –

my dripping

desire

the salt

Square Holes

My body's
in–being
aches for her
fertile silence
now naked
now revealed
staring back
unashamed
each time
a different
shape
each time
a different
name
full breasted
or small, waist
wan or fertile
full–hipped
full–lipped
or slender
with brown eyes
that mellow or
green/blue that chill
or black orbs
beckoning darkly
sucking my soul

William Driscoll

in like an ecstasy

a momentary

torment of

sweat and regret

Change is a woman

not a girl

experienced, savvy

who knows how to

be a woman

who culls her lovers

with a scythe

with a smile

merciless and

alluring

Trinity

Your mind is soft
in life, pliable
my mind is water
wearing down stone
seeking a level
filling low places
our minds grow hard
in death, rigid
our minds are dead leaves
crumbling to earth

Your heart is beating
in life, shrieking
my heart is fire
burning away emptiness
warming cold places
soldering connections
our hearts grow still
in death, silent
our hearts are ashes
blackening our hands

Your soul is light
in life, bu'yant

William Driscoll

my soul's a day–dream

calling me to waken

flickering dark places

lightening my fetters

our souls never die

just sink, crusted

our souls are nightmares

plaguing our sleep

The Martyrdom of Celcilia

...consumed – black ash

dim as embered memory

writ large as a winter sky – en–

cased in a gray–green calcified urn

unturned till this_October

not April is cruel to me cruel –

to me unendingly hateful and

depraved_of sense and senses

senseless_limed–white – dull

the decay of flesh unfleshed

by bitter – bitter years –

in a disquiet ground –

ice winds the heart –

a hollowed sound_arrested – a

bow on a bridge without

strings_achingly – dull and empty

still_silently she owns me

still_holds me with her beauty

still_patience and accusing peace–

fulness_to kill – her peace again –

to slice open her agony_anew

to squeeze her tighter – to feel her

near_again to ignore her – smile

as she frowns my insensitivity my

uselessness – my depravity – my restless–

anger – my hopelessness_end me

with her acid–faith again – tender

skinned to raw–red pulp exposed

open and open – how she holds me

with her memory

tighter than any chain

she returns again and again

and again and I

remain – consumed...

xvii

When ga puts 'is finga on ya

com' on don

com' on don

when ga puts dat finga on ya

ra ra ra

ain't notin' gonna matter to ya

ra ra ra

when ga puts dat finga on ya

com' on don

com' on don

Dats m' luv in dat steel ya say

com' on don

com' on don

dats m' luv in dat steel dar

ra ra ra

sixty emphas twisty way ya say

com' on don

com' on don

sixty emphas den tall twisty dar

ra ra ra

Po–lice is sayin' back 'way 'way

com' on don

com' on don

dats m' luv in dat steel dar

ra ra ra

dats 'er blud ah dat steel dar

ra ra ra

Dare ain't no troubles in da wirl ya say

com' on don

com' on don

dare ain't no trouble in da wirl at all

ra ra ra

da pur dey–ain't–hunga in dare tums

da even so ain't darin' mo

when ga puts dat finga on ya

ra ra ra

For Michael, 2000

i

As I left them they were dancing
to the varied strain, a music
dim and daunting, a balance
of knife points on finger tips
a lulling that belayed the hour

How could such a slender hand
as this? petite and white with
rings of such delight and sparkle
how could such a tiny arm?
perfumed, powdered and petite
oh, how could such a lovely voice?

Out damn spot!
Out!

Duncan bleeds, bloody mouths
that tell the tale red

Duncan bleeds – so
how should I proceed?

ii

As I went out, it was mourning
chill, icy and they were dancing
for the world mourning
lost sentences and flowering songs
a fable of strength unbounded

Aeneas strode among them
bold and certain
and the ladies bent
like pond reeds
son of Anchises sailing
from their shores
sailing, sailing…

Lament, lost Carthage
Dido sings her last lament

Dido sings her last lament – so
what should I present?

iii

The sea is a quiet grave
the earth, its sister
moist and busy
such waters whisper flesh

from bone, tall or short
all mass and girth are scrimshawed
by their dampened touch

And there lies Pallas who sought
dour Turnus' arms

Where bound, Aeneas?
Where bound?

And there lies Dido
with consecrated grain
in her pure hands
her dress ungirdled
her hair unbraided
her love, sharp as lies
pointed 'gainst her breast
with bitter enmity

I die unavenged, she cries,
but let me die

Sew salt, embattled dancers

Aeneas has sailed toward
his destined plume

William Driscoll

Aeneas has sailed toward his

destined plume – so

how should I presume?

xix

"Black corners of winter, whom do you pine for?"

I luv a girl with a way with words
(though these be often sad and lost)
A bluish ice, a winter frost
A silence in the songs of birds

Still beneath the bending lines
That labor in a darkened room
They burst like sunshine on a bloom
That heliotropes this field of tine

And with a verb they'll caress your
    being
And bring a note of sadness in
With metaphor they sin and sin
Then claim that it was all a fling

When on a preposition they pause –
(until it seems you're going mad) –
Then with repetition sad
And heathen without cause

They catch you in a turn of phrase
There hold you in their lover's hands

William Driscoll

Until the time that you must part
And shuffle back to the moriband

Prayer One: The Demiurge

You are the light and I am the eye.

You are the wind that wakes the twigs in spring.

The buds. The growth of buds. The blossom.

You are the crack of ice and hoarfrost.

The release of icicles and sheaves.

Small birds. Green birch leaves.

The bush of red foxtail in the brush.

I see you in the full mooned sky white with clouds.

The degree of rain upon an ocher lake at sunrise.

You are mist, quickening and hunger –

aurora, lightning and spring rain.

You are the blue rivulet to my ice–pond –

(the scutter to my narcolept – the caffeine to my anodyne).

You warm the earth and send me

shooting forth to fight the sky

"and I hate you and fear you and look for you everywhere
with dread."

www.ingramcontent.com/pod-product-compliance
Lightning Source LLC
Chambersburg PA
CBHW060625030426
42337CB00018B/3207